Contemporary Issues

Facing Family Crises

Caring and Coping

Girl Scouts of the U.S.A.
830 Third Avenue
New York, N.Y. 10022

 GIRL SCOUTS OF THE U.S.A.

Betty F. Pilsbury, *National President*
Frances Hesselbein, *National Executive Director*

Inquiries related to *Contemporary Issues: Caring and Coping* should be directed to Program, Girl Scouts of the U.S.A., 830 Third Avenue, New York, N.Y. 10022.

Author: Harriet S. Mosatche, Ph.D.
Contributors: Verna Simpkins
　　　　　　　Karen Unger-Sparks

This publication may not be reproduced, stored in a retrieval system, or transmitted in whole or in part or by any means, electronic or mechanical, photocopying, recording, or otherwise, without the prior written permission of Girl Scouts of the United States of America, 830 Third Avenue, New York, N.Y. 10022.

© 1988 by Girl Scouts of the United States of America
All rights reserved
First Impression 1988
Printed in the United States of America
5 4

ISBN 0-88441-465-5

Contents

Introduction	5
The Scope of Family Crises Today	5
Divorce and Remarriage	6
A Death in the Family	9
Poverty and Hunger	10
Homelessness	11
Specific Tips for Girl Scout Leaders	12
Suggested Troop/Group Activities to Help Girls Understand and Cope with Family Crises	14
Daisy Girl Scout Activities	14
Brownie Girl Scout Activities	15
Junior Girl Scout Activities	16
Cadette Girl Scout Activities	17
Senior Girl Scout Activities	18
Program Links	19
Resources	20

The Girl Scout Contemporary Issues Series

Tune In to Well-Being, Say No to Drugs: Substance Abuse

Staying Safe: Preventing Child Abuse

Girls Are Great: Growing Up Female

Into the World of Today and Tomorrow: Leading Girls to Mathematics, Science, and Technology

Reaching Out: Preventing Youth Suicide

Caring and Coping: Facing Family Crises

Decisions for Your Life: Preventing Teenage Pregnancy

Earth Matters: A Challenge for Environmental Action

Valuing Differences: Pluralism

Right to Read: Literacy

Introduction

In the United States today, many families face a variety of serious personal, social, and economic crises. Even those children who do not directly feel the impact of family problems probably have friends, classmates, and relatives who have experienced difficulties as a result of these crises. Since children who have strong support networks deal best with the stresses that beset them, Girl Scouting can play an important role in helping youngsters understand and cope with family crises, whether these occur in their own households or in the homes of friends and acquaintances.

This booklet will focus on four particularly prevalent family crises—divorce, a death in the family, poverty and hunger, and homelessness. These crises profoundly affect millions of children in their personal, social, mental, and academic development. The information and activities in this booklet are provided to enable Girl Scout leaders to increase their efforts both in helping girls become aware of some common family stresses and in assisting girls in handling those serious family problems that personally touch their lives.

The Scope of Family Crises Today

Below are some statistics that demonstrate how widespread these family crises are at the present time:

■ By age 18, more than one-third of this nation's children will experience their parents' divorce, and perhaps as many as 20 percent will be involved in a second divorce some time later.

■ Only 73 percent of White, 67 percent of Hispanic, and 38 percent of Black children live with both biological parents. Approximately 42 percent of White and 86 percent of Black children are likely to spend at least some time in a single-parent household.

■ More than 1,000 stepfamilies are formed each day. Over 6 million children under the age of 18 live in a household with a stepparent, with many other children spending at least some time living with a stepparent.

■ In 1985, 3.6 percent of the children in the United States under the age of 18 had lost one or both parents by death. About 1,699,000 children had lost a father, 599,000 had lost a mother, and 33,000 were totally orphaned.

■ In 1989, 12.6 million children were poor, approximately 20 percent of all children under the age of 18. The largest group of poor Americans is children under the age of three. Overall, young people account for 40 percent of the nation's poor.

■ More than 100,000 children die each year as a direct result of poverty. The rate of child poverty in the United States is more than three times that of other economically advanced nations. Fewer than 9 percent of the nation's poor live in core cities: 28 percent live in the suburbs and the largest number live in semi-isolation in small towns and rural areas.

- Two-thirds of the nation's poor are White. It is estimated that one White child in seven is poor. Four out of nine African-American children are poor, while three out of eight Hispanic children are poor. Moreover, 56 percent of families headed by single Black women and 59 percent of families headed by single Hispanic women are poor. Nearly half of all poor children do not receive Medicaid benefits.

- Estimates of the homeless population in the United States range from 600,000 people to 3 million people. Homeless mothers and their children are the fastest growing percentage of the nation's homeless population. An estimated 43 percent of homeless children do not attend school.

- One in twelve Americans experiences hunger at least some days each month, approximately 20 million people. Nearly 1.5 million children are malnourished.

- According to the Children's Defense Fund estimates based on 1987 figures, the cost of eliminating child poverty is over $17 billion and the cost of eliminating poverty among all Americans is over $50 billion—a staggering amount, yet only 1 percent of the gross national product of the United States and only 15 percent of what has been earmarked to bail out the savings and loan industry. (Kappan Special Report: "Children of Poverty, The Status of 12 Million Young Americans." Bloomington, Ind.: June 1990.)

Divorce and Remarriage

While the divorce rate in the United States has leveled off recently, and appears to have even begun to drop, over 1 million children each year still face the divorce or separation of their parents. Many factors determine how well children adjust to the breakup of their parents' marriage, and not all children react in a similar fashion. While the majority of parents feel that divorce has improved their lives, most also feel that the marital dissolution has had an adverse impact on their children. Mothers and fathers are often concerned that in creating more happiness for themselves, they are causing psychological damage to their daughters and sons. While it is true that an intact family marked by constant conflict, tension, and verbal abuse can harm children, divorce and separation are always major upheavals.

Divorce is not the only family trauma that is beyond the children's control. Increasingly, single, unmarried females are becoming heads of households, with a father never being a part of the family portrait. Moreover, there has been an increased rate of desertion in which the parents do not divorce, but in which one parent abdicates all responsibility for the children. Statistically, children from families that are headed by a female are more likely to be poor, homeless, hungry, ill, and socially maladjusted. These children not only suffer all the shocks of divorce, but also experience an enormous set of additional problems.

For those children who perceived their parents as happy together, adjustment to divorce is much more difficult than for those children who viewed the preseparation period as an unhappy time for everyone. In some instances, as a mother or father becomes the kind of caring parent she or he couldn't be previously because of the tension in the home, children benefit from the family reorganization. And if one parent has been physically or emotionally abusive, children are frequently openly relieved by the departure of that parent.

Upon first learning of an impending divorce, a child's reaction may be shock. Once they begun to accept the reality of the situation, children usually experience deep grief and depression. These emotions are sometimes expressed indirectly—perhaps as accident proneness or rebellious behavior such as lying or stealing. In time, anger and bitterness may replace the sadness. Some youngsters become destructive or aggressive, venting their frustration on their possessions, peers, or parents.

Some children react physically to the stress of divorce, developing nausea, vomiting, loss of appetite, headaches, or asthma attacks. Other children show lower academic achievement and higher rates of absenteeism and lateness. Doing poorly in school may result from an inability to concentrate; or it may be a conscious or unconscious way to punish parents for the pain they have caused.

Children react to divorce with varying degrees and types of distress, depending on their age. While preschoolers may initially be more emotional, they seem to adapt faster than older children. However, young children often respond to the separation from a parent with denial, asking repeatedly, "When is Daddy coming back?" or "Why isn't Mommy here?" By five or six, children are usually capable of understanding what happens in a divorce, but many still fantasize about the missing parent's return. They need reassurance that they will not be abandoned and will continue to be loved by both parents. This reassurance may come from a strong, loving relationship with a grandparent, aunt, uncle, or other family member.

Elementary school-age children are concerned about having to move away from friends or start in a new school. They worry about where the noncustodial parent will live and whether they will see her or him. It is a time of intense sadness and powerlessness for them. Adolescents often manifest the damaging effects of divorce most openly. Running away from home, stealing, substance abuse, sexual activity, even suicide attempts are some of the ways they can cry out for attention and express their distress. After divorce, children are forced to deal not only with their own feelings of loss, but they must also cope with the sadness and confusion their parents are experiencing. In some instances, teenagers virtually lose their childhood when their parents divorce. They become the main source of emotional support for their siblings and their parents, and take on many of the responsibilities of the absent parent. While this new role may increase the self-esteem of some youngsters, others find themselves unable to cope and feel overburdened and angry. They sometimes blame themselves and ask questions like, "What did I do?" or "What could I have done to keep them together?"

The sex of the child is another important factor to consider when gauging the effects of divorce. It has been well-documented that boys exhibit more overt and recognizable reactions to divorce than do girls. For instance, while studies have often found no difference in school achievement between girls from two-parent and single-parent homes, father absence through divorce has generally been associated with lower grades for boys. However, some researchers speculate that while girls are likely to be as troubled as boys by marital conflict and divorce, they display less withdrawal or anxiety or other kinds of psychological pain. Sometimes boys appear to exhibit behavior problems long before a divorce becomes final, but girls may not manifest their emotional turmoil until years after a divorce, perhaps not until adolescence. Daughters from divorced families have more negative attitudes about marriage and are often afraid of being betrayed by boyfriends or husbands. There is evidence that some girls from divorced families may be likely to be overly flirtatious, to be sexually active at an early age, to marry young, to be unhappy with their own spouses, and ultimately to get divorced themselves. When fathers continue to play an active role in a girl's life, these differences are less likely to occur.

Parental attitudes and actions before and after the divorce help determine a child's adjustment to it. To prevent children from believing that they are responsible for the divorce, they need to be given as much information as possible in a straightforward manner about the circumstances surrounding the marriage breakup. However, placing blame or providing very personal details is not advisable. Even very young children need to be prepared for the departure of a parent and to be told where they will live and who will take care of them. In some cases, children are used as pawns in a continuing struggle between the parents, and youngsters may learn to play one side against the other. When the postdivorce relationship between the parents allows both of them to show love and interest consistently, when there is a regular visitation schedule by the noncustodial parent, when parents communicate about practical matters related to the children and have consistent rules for them, their adjustment is most successful.

Typically, children live with their mothers after divorce, although more and more parents today are opting for joint custody in which legal responsibility for the children is shared. Some family therapists are concerned that joint custody may mean a partial commitment to the child. It may also introduce complications caused by the physical disruptions necessitated by the child having more than one home environment. However, at its best, this arrangement can encourage the noncustodial parent to play a more active role in the child's life. Some research studies have found that children living in the custody of the parent of the same sex were better adjusted than children living with the opposite-sex parent. This may be why girls generally seem to fare better in divorce situations.

Children adjust to divorce at different rates; even children in the same family may respond differently to the family reorganization. Most children eventually cope, but some do become long-term victims, unable to adjust successfully to the family crisis. The passage of time usually allows healing to take place; children observed three years after divorce are remarkably different from those seen just a few months or a year after the divorce. In the first year after the breakup, routines are often disrupted—meals are unplanned, bath and bed times become irregular, and discipline is haphazard. Children frequently move away from friends, live in a new home, and attend a new school. Unfortunately, the trend is for divorced fathers to generally become less and less available to their children as time goes by. While boys often continue to show academic, social, and behavioral problems two years after divorce, girls do considerably better, becoming much more like their peers from two-parent homes by this time.

Even though divorce causes pain and anxiety for all family members, many single parents discover hidden strengths and find satisfaction in new areas of their lives. Children often become more responsible and mature. Eventually, parents begin to date again, and many marry. Some children are relieved to see a parent less lonely and having fun again, while others resent the new person who seems to be replacing their other parent. Remarriage is least negative for children younger than eight, and most difficult for teenagers, while children between about 8 and 12 respond somewhere in between. Most children experience some degree of anxiety about how the new family situation will affect their lives. They may have to share their home and possessions not only with a new stepparent, but with stepsiblings as well. Their position in the family may change too, perhaps from being the "baby" to being a middle child. Expecting an easy and fast adjustment will result in frustration and disappointment for everyone. In those instances in which a noncustodial parent begins to spend less and less time with her or his children, while becoming more involved with her or his new spouse's family, the children are bound to be deeply hurt.

Some children respond to remarriage by becoming withdrawn, disruptive in school, neglectful of their academic work, or by running away. The message to children needs to be that the new family member will not be frightened away regardless of the tactics employed by the children. Children need to know that their feelings are being considered, but they should never be placed in the position of making the decision about remarriage. That is the responsibility of the adults only. In some cases, children are afraid to get too close to a stepparent for fear that she or he will abandon them later on, or they may feel that any sign of loyalty or love shown toward a stepparent is a betrayal of the absent parent.

The best adjustment is usually made when children are adequately prepared for the changes in their lives and when they have been given ample opportunities to become acquainted with their future stepparent. When the remarriage does not threaten their close relationship with the noncustodial parent and grandparents, children have an easier time. The new stepparent needs to develop a relationship with the children gradually, rather than trying to take control of the family abruptly. The attachment between stepparents and stepchildren can be a positive and significant one. Finding better ways to communicate and doing enjoyable, interesting activities together can help to cement the bonds of the reconstituted or blended family.

A Death in the Family

A death or permanent disability occurring to someone close to a person, whether a parent, grandparent, sibling, close relative, friend, or guardian, or even a pet, is tragic at any age, but even more devastating when it happens during childhood or adolescence. It takes a period of time before the full impact of the loss becomes a reality, particularly when a death of a family member is sudden. Young children often continue to hope and even expect that the parent will return, as if she or he were just on a trip. One of the reasons remarriage is so painful for a child whose parent has died is that she is then often forced to give up that fantasy. A sense of personal vulnerability often emerges after the death of a parent. Children ask themselves, "Could this happen to me?" They need help in differentiating themselves from the dead parent, particularly if it is a parent of the same sex who has died. Children often express concerns, sometimes indirectly, about the health of the surviving parent. "Will my mother (or father) die also?" is the thought most on their minds. Even a minor illness such as a cold might seem catastrophic to a child already touched by the tragedy of one parent's death.

Whenever there is a family tragedy, a child may feel abandoned and may even feel responsible in some way. Although a child needs and wants to be loved, she may become hostile, aggressive, or withdrawn. Some children react by regressing to an earlier stage in life. Becoming a baby again can simultaneously dull the intense pain of loss and deny the inevitability of growing up and dying.

In many instances, the child's grieving is delayed because of the necessity of dealing with such matters as changed child-care arrangements or moving to a new home. Moreover, young children are often excluded from the formal mourning process by well-meaning relatives, friends, or neighbors. Adults frequently assume that the less said about death, the more protected the child will be from the harsh reality of the loss. But a child's feelings, even at a young age, are intense, and while her understanding of death may be incomplete, the enormity of the event will certainly be comprehended. Thus, a child who is taken out for a day of fun at the amusement park while her parent is being buried may later feel confused, guilty, and rejected. Children can cope better with the open sadness of family members than with the silence of deception.

Adolescents are generally more able than children to cope with death. Intellectually, socially, and emotionally, they are better prepared for death and its aftermath. They can play a meaningful role in the funeral or other memorial services and can reach out to friends, teachers, clergy, and youth leaders for support. However, adolescent girls whose fathers died while the girls were children tend to be shy and uncomfortable around males and often anxious about sexual matters.

When a parent is lost through death or divorce, the support of the remaining parent is sorely needed by the children just at a time when that parent is undergoing her own intense personal crisis. It is crucial that the surviving parent reach out to the child in any way she or he can. Sharing feelings and memories can help the grieving child put her own feelings of loss into words and develop a realistic, rather than idealized, image of the deceased parent. Sharing family beliefs regarding death and an afterlife may also be a source of comfort to the child.

Even years after a parent's death, the child may continue to mourn her great loss and experience the effects of the tragedy. Hearing the words of a song or seeing someone who reminds her of her parent can bring back the pain.

While the death of a pet does not compare in severity to the death of a parent, the loss of a beloved dog or cat is often a child's first experience with death and separation. Children under the age of five are especially likely to believe that they caused the pet to die. Older children may try to protect themselves from death by calling the dead pet names or expressing hatred for it. Adolescents may hide their grief, but can be particularly upset when a pet that has been in the family a long time dies. Parents should allow the child to express her sadness in her own way. A child can also be encouraged to create a memorial for the pet. Parents can share their own feelings of grief with their children. This lets the child know that her feelings are acceptable.

Poverty and Hunger

Poverty is a reality for increasingly more women and girls. More than half of the poor population in the United States of America is accounted for by single mothers and their children. One widely disseminated report suggested that in the first year after divorce, women's income declined considerably while men's income increased. Millions of mothers receive little or no child support payments, and, in many instances, court-ordered payments to custodial mothers are insufficient to meet family needs. Research suggests that some problems in children assumed to be related to the absence of the father may actually be the result of economic hardship.

Poverty exerts both direct and indirect effects on youngsters. Malnutrition and hunger, decreased resistance to disease, physical and mental underdevelopment, and constant psychological stress are just some of the burdens placed on children by poverty. A hungry child will find it harder to concentrate in school. A family in which parents are struggling to find work, or in which parents are working two or three jobs just to get by, will have less time to spend with a child—to play, to help her with her homework, or to read her a bedtime story. A child's study time might be spent caring for younger siblings. Her environment might be too noisy or stressful to allow her to study or the child might never have been taught the value of school and good grades.

Studies have reported that poor children receive lower average scores on intelligence tests and poorer grades in school. Their language skills, as measured by traditional testing methods, often appear to lag behind those of middle-class children. Intelligence and standardized tests are written for the "average" middle-class child who comes from an enriched environment and whose family's values emphasize preschool education and educational-type play, such as alphabet blocks, slateboards, or coloring books. A label of slow or underachiever is then attached to a child from an early age and becomes just one more burden for her to overcome. Some children, unfortunately, never reach their full potential. They believe the label placed upon them and stop struggling.

Poor families often lack access to resources that can potentially provide support in times of crises. The income gap between families with the highest incomes and families with the lowest incomes was wider in 1988 than in any year since 1947. Poorer families have also been hurt by the change from a manufacturing economy to a service economy. Service industry jobs pay less than manufacturing jobs, often paying little more than minimum wage, and sometimes have no medical benefits. In the past, a high school graduate could work in manufacturing and expect to earn enough over her lifetime to support a family. Today, if the wage earner of a family of four worked a 40-hour week with no vacation for a total year at a service job that pays a higher than minimum wage rate of $5.40 an hour, she would still be at the poverty line.

Eighty-seven percent of poor children live in a family in which at least one person is employed some part of the time. The general assumption that people are poor because they don't work hard enough or because they are lazy is not proven by statistics and facts. What is tragic is that adults, with inadequate support networks, may pass their frustrations and feelings of hopelessness and incompetence to their children.

When families suddenly find themselves in poverty due to unemployment, every member is affected. Since our society places so much value on work, previously employed individuals find themselves depressed and with decreased self-esteem. The children in the family learn to feel helpless and inadequate by observing parental role models who exhibit these characteristics.

Family disorganization is not typical of every disadvantaged family. In many such families, children are cared for and taught in an organized, stimulating home with regular schedules and rules. Children growing up in such circumstances are able effectively to relate to and communicate with others and to learn more in school and other learning environments.

Just as families differ in their response to life conditions, children respond in different ways to the circumstances of their lives. Research has discovered that certain children seem to be incredibly resilient, allowing them to cope effectively with even the harshest reality. These exceptional children are self-confident, independent, achievement-oriented, and socially adept. It has been found that a particular inspirational adult often figures prominently in the lives of these strong children. That one person might be a parent or grandparent but could just as well be a member of the clergy, a teacher, a friend's parent, or a Girl Scout leader—anyone with whom a child can identify and who can help a child develop confidence and a sense of future accomplishment.

Homelessness

The stresses that children who are poor face every day double for those who are homeless. Since 1980, federal assistance for low-income housing has decreased by 76 percent; the cost of housing has soared; and the only jobs that are increasing in number are low-paying. It is estimated that over 1 million children and young people live "on the streets" in the course of a year.

If the basic needs of people are examined—shelter, food, water, a feeling of safety and security, and a sense of belonging—homelessness destroys these most basic of requirements for intellectual and emotional growth. A homeless child will find it almost impossible to progress to feelings of self-esteem and self-actualization, concern and love for others, and pride in her culture if she is not sure where and to whom or to what she belongs.

The stress caused by homelessness affects the health and intellect, as well as the creativity and emotional well-being of children and youth. School adds stress if a child has fallen behind due to constantly moving; if she is mocked as the "homeless" kid; if she is hungry, sleepy, rejected, or isolated. Research has shown that children as young as nine months recognize the expectation of failure. By nine months, a child's sense of self-worth can be dulled to the point that the child expects no praise or reward for any of the most simple of successes.

Early intervention as well as increased parental and adult involvement can make a difference. A Girl Scout leader who accepts each girl and praises her individual strengths can have a marvelous impact on a child. Children need to be taught not to lose their innate humanity and compassion. A Girl Scout leader also has the power to increase the empathy and understanding of those girls in her troop/group who are not poor and who are not homeless and to emphasize that these crises profoundly affect all children, young people, and adults.

Specific Tips for Girl Scout Leaders

As a caring, trusted Girl Scout leader with an established relationship with the girls in your troop or group, you are in an ideal position to help girls whose lives have been disrupted by family crises. Unlike a parent or other family member who is directly involved in a crisis situation, you are removed enough to offer calm reassurance and support.

You can also provide the kind of environment that will help girls not directly faced with serious family problems to act with understanding and sensitivity toward those who are dealing with them. Here are some tips:

- Provide an atmosphere of openness, freedom, and trust so that girls will feel comfortable expressing themselves, asking questions, and seeking advice.

- Encourage play and other kinds of physical activity as a natural way for girls to release the tensions associated with family crises and to distract them temporarily from their problems.

- Learn to recognize when to draw a girl out for conversation about something that is troubling her and when to leave her alone with her thoughts.

- Recognize that there are times when peer support is needed and other times when an experienced adult would provide greater comfort to a girl.

- Demonstrate an accepting, nonjudgmental attitude about different family situations.

- Be aware of each girl's home situation so you can understand her problems and extend a helping hand. However, respect the privacy of the girl and her family. Don't pry unnecessarily for details about her family situation.

- Encourage girls going through difficult times at home to continue to attend meetings and participate in troop/group activities. These meetings can lend stability to a child's troubled world.

- Be sensitive to the fact that many girls with whom you have contact may be from single-parent families, poor families, or homeless families.

- Help girls take action to reduce or eliminate minor stresses to lessen their feelings of powerlessness in the face of family problems they cannot solve.

- Show each girl that you think she is important and that you are concerned about her welfare.

- Look for strengths in girls rather than for weaknesses. Help girls see that they can solve problems.

- Help girls to express their anger in ways that do not alienate friends and others who want to support them.

- Be aware that family stress does not always have a negative impact on children. Being forced to deal with problems can provide children with the impetus for developing problem-solving, coping, and social skills.

- Recognize that when girls are consistently quiet, unquestioning, and too well-behaved, they may not be coping well with a family crisis. Help them to express their concerns and feelings.

- Recognize that each girl responds differently to a family crisis. Some may act depressed while others will become aggressive.

- Recognize that even girls in two-parent families feel the burden of divorce and parental death when these crises touch the lives of their close friends.

- Be aware that many children in stable homes worry about the possibility of divorce when they hear their parents fight.

- Be sensitive to the fact that a girl's religious beliefs may affect how her family deals with problems, particularly divorce and death.

- Praise and encourage signs of cooperation in stepsisters who are in the same troop/group rather than focusing on their conflicts.

- Be sensitive when planning activities that either require both parents to attend or that specify which parent is to attend—for example, a mother/daughter weekend or a dad/daughter dinner.

- Be sensitive when planning activities with your troop/group. Not every child may be able to contribute baked goods or other foods, or materials needed for activities. In some situations, it may be better not to do the activity than to call attention to a child's situation or to ask others to "help her out."

- Be aware that when planning field trips or events, some girls may not have the transportation, resources, or clothing to be able to participate. Offers to help subsidize a girl's costs could be resented. Try to find some way in which all girls can be on an equal footing.

- Be sensitive to making statements that assume that all girls share similar backgrounds, housing arrangements, or family situations. Girls may not have a bedroom in which to hang their collage or a parent for whom they can make a Mother's Day gift. Be especially sensitive around holidays when gifts are exchanged—birthdays or religious and cultural celebrations. Some girls may not have received gifts or may have received few gifts.

- Acknowledge alternate methods of contributing to community service efforts or the Juliette Low World Friendship Fund. Asking each girl to contribute 50 pennies, for example, may not be possible. Working as a troop/group might be more equitable. Be aware, when describing service activities, that certain words may be hurtful to some girls in the troop/group—e.g., "helping those poor, struggling people."

- Remember that special arrangements may have to be made for Girl Scout events when both divorced parents and perhaps stepparents plan to attend. Try to avoid situations in which the hostility of the adults may ruin the day for a girl.

- Let girls know they are free to love both parents, even if one has moved away from home.

- Be aware that a girl may be too embarrassed to tell you directly that she can't afford dues, recognitions, special fees, or a uniform. Be sensitive to her feelings in the manner in which help is offered.

- Encourage parents to participate in troop/group activities related to family crises.

- Find out about agencies in your community that can help girls and their families in crisis situations.

- Try to keep in touch with girls who move to another location.

Suggested Troop/Group Activities to Help Girls Understand and Cope with Family Crises

As a Girl Scout leader, you will want to focus on activities that promote understanding of and sensitivity about contemporary family crises as part of your ongoing program. Girls at all age levels, in partnership with Girl Scout leaders, can gain an awareness of some family problems that are widespread in our society today.

The following recommended activities are designed to help girls understand the nature of family issues and to recognize that all families go through difficult times. Some activities will assist girls in knowing how to cope with their own family problems by helping them to develop problem-solving, stress management, and communication skills. Other activities can provide girls with information about working with others and finding out where to get help in their communities.

The Caring and Coping patch is available to girls from Brownie through Senior Girl Scout age levels who participate in "Facing Family Crises" activities. Information on ordering the patch is available from your council.

Daisy Girl Scout Activities

Daisy Girl Scouts can begin to understand the different kinds of families and also learn that people and strategies can ease the problems families experience. Daisy Girl Scouts can participate in the following activities:

1. Help girls understand that there are many different kinds of families. For example, one child may live with her mother and see her father on some weekends only, while another child lives with her father, stepmother, and stepbrothers.

2. Help girls understand what it means to be poor by sharing their thoughts and feelings. Be sure to be sensitive to girls' feelings about their family situations.

3. Have girls care for an animal such as a fish that has a short life cycle so that they can learn what death means.

4. Ask girls to think about people they could go to for help in dealing with a problem at home. Encourage them to list trusted adults like relatives, clergy, teachers, and Girl Scout leaders.

5. Have girls suggest fun activities they can do for free. Girls can then select one or two of these activities to carry out. Keep in mind costs like transportation and snacks.

6. Help girls make up a song about the meaning of family. Have them sing the song as a group.

7. Have girls prepare a list of active games that can help relieve the stress caused by family problems. Play some of these games.

8. Have girls think of some enjoyable activities they can do to reduce the stress brought on by family situations over which they have no control.

9. Help the girls discover what their calorie and nutrition needs are for their age, height, and weight. Plan some daily menus that would include the foods that Daisy Girl Scouts need for proper growth. Girls can contribute healthy recipes for a group cookbook, plan a week or monthly calendar of meals, make a poster or chart of healthy foods and how they help Daisy Girl Scouts grow (e.g., dairy products provide calcium, etc.), or make a group promise to try to eat less junk food.

Brownie Girl Scout Activities

Brownie Girl Scouts can learn about some of the problems families face today. They can also begin to develop sensitivity to the feelings of girls who must deal with problems such as divorce or poverty. Brownie Girl Scouts can participate in the following activities:

1. Make a poster on the theme "My Family." It can include words, photographs, and drawings.

2. Share ideas about what you could do to help out at home if your mother or father lost her or his job. You might try doing one or more of these chores even if there has been no job loss.

3. Find pictures that show different kinds of families doing a variety of things. For example, a grandfather works in the garden with his grandchildren; a father and mother play with their child in the park; a grandmother, mother, and teenager prepare dinner together; and a father drives his baby to a day-care center. Make a families montage with the pictures.

4. Invite a social worker or family therapist to talk to your troop or group about sad things that may happen in families and how girls can deal with these problems.

5. Learn what the words divorce, custody, unemployment, homelessness, hunger, and poverty mean.

6. In a group, discuss what you would do if your best friend told you about a big problem in her family.

7. Using dolls or puppets, put on skits about:

- a happy family experience
- a sad family event
- a funny family experience

8. Think of some hobbies or activities you can do when you're feeling upset. Your list might include dancing, drawing, reading, talking to a friend, or playing a special game. Remember this list when something bothers you.

9. As a group, discuss ways to make sure every girl can be included in all troop or group events regardless of cost. Be sure to be sensitive to girls' feelings about their family situations.

10. Brainstorm ideas about how family members can get along better with each other. Try out some of these ideas.

11. Find out if your community has a food bank, a community garden, or food co-op. See what you can do as a troop/group to help.

12. Make a list of the five favorite activities that you do with your family or with your friends. Put a star next to each of the activities that are free. As a troop/group, try to think of as many activities as possible that are fun and that do not cost money to do. Try to do at least one of these activities each week.

Junior Girl Scout Activities

Junior Girl Scouts can learn about family crises through books, television, and music. They can also find out about family support services and agencies in their communities. Junior Girl Scouts can participate in the following activities:

1. Make a collage that shows family members helping each other during hard times.

2. Read a book about a single-parent family. What were the positive and/or negative effects of this family situation on the children?

3. Watch a television program or see a movie that shows how family members cope with being poor.

4. Find out about careers devoted to working with troubled families. For example, find out what is required to become a social worker, a family therapist, or a psychiatrist.

5. Make posters publicizing family support services in your area. Include telephone numbers and addresses. Find out where these posters can be displayed. Check places like schools, libraries, churches, synagogues, and stores.

6. As a group, brainstorm about the wide variety of family groups that live in our country today—for example, single parents, stepfamilies, traditional families, and extended families.

7. Invite a professional from a family service agency to talk to your troop or group about family problems. Ask her or him to talk about ways to reduce feelings of tension. Include a question-and-answer period.

8. Learn how to help a friend who has been touched deeply by a sad family event such as a serious illness of a brother or sister or a divorce. Role-play what you might say to her. If she needs more help than you can give her, find out where she might go.

9. With your troop or group, brainstorm a list of sports and fitness activities Daisy and Brownie Girl Scouts can do that cost little or no money. Share this list with the troops and groups in your community.

10. Organize a session in which girls sing songs about family issues. Be sure to include some songs that are upbeat and have positive messages. The songs can be popular hits, old songs, or ones made up especially for this event. Listen carefully to the words of each song and discuss its message.

11. Think of some things you might do to improve communication in your family. Try one of your ideas for at least one week.

12. Find out the official United States poverty line for a family of four. Make a chart of how you would spend that money on housing, food, clothing, and other necessities. Look at your community. How much do houses cost, apartment rentals, food, etc.? How much money do you think you would need each year to live comfortably?

13. Participate in planning or serving a holiday meal at a shelter or food kitchen. What else can your troop/group do to help?

14. Interview your school cafeteria officials to find out how much food your school wastes each week. Or, keep track of how much food your family wastes each week. What can you do to help waste less food?

Cadette Girl Scout Activities

Cadette Girl Scouts can develop their awareness of the effect of family crises on children. They can also find out how to help individuals in their community who must deal directly with the effects of hunger, divorce, and other serious problems. Cadette Girl Scouts can participate in the following activities:

1. Find out what children's books are available in your local library that deal with family problems such as death, divorce, or poverty. Make a list that includes titles, age levels, and subjects. Share this list with members of troops/groups of Brownie, Junior, and Cadette Girl Scouts.

2. With a group, put on a play that dramatizes a family crisis.

3. Write a fairy tale that has a *good* stepparent as a main character (unlike the ones that are usually found in fairy tales such as "Cinderella" or "Snow White"). Share it with younger children as a story or puppet show.

4. Put together a brochure describing support services available in your community for children whose parents have recently separated or divorced, or compile a "kid survival" guide with free or inexpensive activities and services that are available in your community.

5. Organize a group service project that works to reduce hunger in your community. You might work with an organization that is already doing something about this issue.

6. Spend time with a younger child who has been separated from a parent through death or divorce.

7. Volunteer to become part of a peer support group at school or in an agency in your community.

8. Invite a family therapist or other mental health professional to come to a troop or group meeting to discuss ways to help family members in crisis situations. Encourage participants to ask questions and voice their concerns.

9. How sensitive are television writers and producers to the reality of family problems? For one week, keep track of how programs and commercials depict family life today. In a discussion group, compare how the media representation compares with everyday life.

10. For a month, keep a diary or personal journal to describe life in your family. Keep it private or just share it with one special friend so that you'll feel free to express your real feelings.

11. Write to a local or national politician to find out what she or he is doing about reducing poverty. Ask what you can do in your community.

12. Find out about diseases caused by malnutrition and poverty. Find out what is being done in your community to help eradicate them.

13. Adopt a room at a homeless shelter or a shelter for battered women. Find out what the residents need. Decorate the room and see what you can do to help.

14. Investigate the causes of homelessness. Find out what is being done at a local level to support homeless families. See what you can do to help in your neighborhood or school.

Senior Girl Scout Activities

Senior Girl Scouts can learn about the statistics on poverty and divorce on a local, national, and international level and they can begin to take action to help those affected by family crises. They can also prepare themselves to cope with the kinds of family problems they may confront in their future. Senior Girl Scouts can participate in the following activities:

1. Find out about the extent of poverty in your community. Have the statistics changed in the last 10 years? How many children are living below the national poverty line? How many children are homeless? What is your community doing to reduce this problem? Decide on a way that you can help.

2. Spend some time with a Daisy or Brownie Girl Scout whose family is going through some kind of crisis.

3. With a small group, develop a board game called Family. Include positive and negative events in the lives of families.

4. Think of ways to encourage a divorced or separated parent to play a larger role in the lives of her or his children. Find out about custody laws in your state. Think about what kinds of changes you'd like to see and how you could make them happen. Act on your ideas.

5. In a group, discuss how you might help a friend or younger girl cope with the death of a parent.

6. Learn about national divorce statistics. Find out how many children in this country have parents who are divorced. How have the figures changed over the past 25 years?

7. Find out about family problems in other cultures. How do they compare to those in the United States? What are some of the similarities and differences in the ways they are handled?

8. Talk to trusted adults who seem to have developed effective strategies for coping with stressful family events. Think about whether any of these strategies might work for you.

9. Organize or participate in a peer counseling group at school to help students cope with serious family problems. Work with a school psychologist, guidance counselor, teacher, or principal.

10. Organize a series of discussions that focus on helping adolescent girls begin to prepare themselves to cope with the kinds of family crises they themselves may face some time in the future. Ask various professionals such as psychologists, family physicians, social workers, matrimonial or family lawyers, clergy, and psychiatrists to present information and answer questions. Keep the group small so that participants will feel comfortable raising questions and concerns.

11. Learn about what divorce mediators, marriage counselors, family therapists, and family or matrimonial lawyers do. Interview people who work in these jobs or write to organizations that represent professionals in these fields.

12. Read newspaper articles about homelessness. How are homeless people portrayed? What are some of the reasons that people are homeless? Create a role-play, skit, or drama using the information you have gathered with homeless people as your characters. Give a performance for younger Girl Scouts.

13. Think about your future. What type of job or career would enable you to lead the kind of life you would most enjoy? Think about what things are important to you. Would you want a house or an apartment? Do you want to live alone or could you have a roommate? What would you need to spend on food, clothing, and other items each month? How much money would you want for entertainment, travel, and other expenses? If you were married, how much money would you need to support two people? to support children? Write down your goals and plans and discuss them in your troop/group.

14. There are many differing opinions on the complex causes of poverty and homelessness. Most people are aware of the damage to children that poverty and homelessness cause. Organize a school or community forum on these issues. Try to collaborate with others in your community on some local solutions and on some national solutions.

Program Links

The following program links provide additional activities and ideas to help girls understand and cope with family crises.

For Daisy Girl Scouts

Daisy Girl Scouts Leaders' Guide
Developmental Characteristics of Daisy Girl Scouts, Working with Daisy Girl Scouts, Daisy Girl Scouts with Special Needs, A Guide to Family Support, The World of Well-Being activities, The World of the Arts activities

For Brownie Girl Scouts

Brownie Girl Scout Handbook
Chapter 2, "About Myself"; Chapter 3, "Taking Care of Myself"; Chapter 4, "People"; Chapter 6, "Things to Know"

More Brownie Girl Scout Try-Its
Caring and Sharing, Manners, Listening to the Past, Her Story, Careers, Good Food, My Body, Me and My Shadow, Outdoor Adventurer

For Junior Girl Scouts

Junior Girl Scout Handbook
Chapter 2, "Who Am I?"; Chapter 3, "Relationships"; Chapter 4, "Decisions, Decisions, Decisions"; Chapter 5, "Leadership and Groups"; Chapter 7, "Day by Day—Skills for Living"; Chapter 8, "Hopes and Dreams"; Chapter 11, Leadership, Looking Your Best, Healthy Living, Careers

Girl Scout Badges and Signs
The World of Well-Being: Across Generations, Becoming a Teen, Caring for Children, Exploring Healthy Eating, Family Living Skills, Health and Fitness, Healthy Relationships, Making Decisions, My Self-Esteem, Safety Sense

The World of People: Celebrating People, Creative Solutions, My Heritage, Women Today, Women's Stories

The World of Today and Tomorrow: Business-Wise, Do-It-Yourself, Money Sense, Ms. Fix-It

The World of the Arts: Books, Communication Arts, Dance, Folk Arts, Jeweler, Photography

The World of the Out-of-Doors: Outdoor Creativity, Outdoor Fun, Outdoor Fun in the City, Walking for Fitness

For Cadette and Senior Girl Scouts

Cadette and Senior Girl Scout Handbook
Chapter 2, "Personal Development"; Chapter 3, "Relationships"; Chapter 5, "Life Skills"; Chapter 6, "From Dreams to Reality: Career Exploration"; Chapter 7, "Citizen of the World"; Chapter 8, "Wider Opportunities"

Cadette and Senior Girl Scout Interest Projects
The World of Well-Being: Child Care, Creative Cooking, Family Living, Fashion/Fitness/Makeup, Managing Stress, Reading, Skills for Living, Tune In to Well-Being

The World of People: Do You Get the Message?, Heritage Hunt, Leadership, Understanding Yourself and Others, Women's History

The World of Today and Tomorrow: Career Exploration, Money Management

The World of the Arts: Artistic Crafts, Creative Writing

The World of the Out-of-Doors: Backpacking, Outdoor Survival

Resources

Consultants: family therapists, social workers, clergy, psychologists, psychiatrists, family or matrimonial lawyers, family physicians

Local groups: family service associations, schools, religious groups, social service agencies, mental health agencies, hospice groups, local bar associations, legal services, self-help groups

National Organizations

American Association for Marriage
  and Family Therapy
1717 K Street, N.W., #407
Washington, D.C. 10006

American Bar Association
750 North Lake Shore Drive
Chicago, Ill. 60611

American Family Therapy Association
2020 Pennsylvania Avenue, N.W., Suite 273
Washington, D.C. 20006

American Orthopsychiatric Association
19 West 44th Street, #1616
New York, N.Y. 10036

American Psychiatric Association
1400 K Street, N.W.
Washington, D.C. 20005

American Psychological Association
1200 17th Street, N.W.
Washington, D.C. 20036

Children's Defense Fund
122 C Street, N.W.
Washington, D.C. 20001

Child Welfare League of America
440 First Street, N.W., Suite 310
Washington, D.C. 20001

Family Resource Coalition
230 North Michigan Avenue
Chicago, Ill. 60601

Family Service America
11700 West Lake Park Drive
Milwaukee, Wis. 53224

Mothers Without Custody
P.O. Box 56762
Houston, Tex. 77256

National Mental Health Association
1021 Prince Street
Alexandria, Va. 22314

National Center for Children in Poverty
Columbia University
154 Haven Avenue, 3rd Floor
New York, N.Y. 10032

National Council for Children's Rights
721 2nd Street, N.E.
Washington, D.C. 20002

National Council on Family Relations
3989 Central Avenue, N.E., Suite 550
Minneapolis, Minn. 55421

National Self-Help Clearinghouse
25 West 43rd Street, Room 620
New York, N.Y. 10036

Parents Without Partners
8807 Colesville Road
Silver Spring, Md. 20910

Remarried Parents, Inc.
c/o Jack Pflaster
102-20 67th Drive
Forest Hills, N.Y. 11375

Stepfamily Association of America
602 East Joppa Road
Baltimore, Md. 21204

Step Family Foundation, Inc.
333 West End Avenue
New York, N.Y. 10023

Books

For Girls

Anders, Rebecca. *A Look at Death*. Minneapolis, Minn.: Lerner, 1977.

Angell, Judie. *What's Best for You?* New York: Dell, 1986.

Arnold, William V. *When Your Parents Divorce*. Philadelphia, Pa.: Westminster, 1980.

Benjamin, Carole L. *The Wicked Stepdog*. New York: Crowell, 1982.

Bernstein, Joanne E. *Loss and How to Cope with It*. New York: Clarion, 1981.

Blume, Judy. *Tiger Eyes*. New York: Dell, 1986.

Bradley, Buff. *Where Do I Belong? A Kids' Guide to Stepfamilies*. Reading, Mass.: Addison-Wesley, 1982.

Bridgers, Sue Ellen. *Notes for Another Life*. New York: Bantam, 1988.

Brown, Margaret Wise. *The Dead Bird*. New York: Dell, 1987.

Buck, Pearl S. *The Big Wave*. New York: Harper & Row, 1986.

Carrick, Carol. *The Accident*. New York: Clarion, 1981.

Childress, Alice. *Rainbow Jordan*. New York: Coward, 1981.

Danzinger, Paula. *The Divorce Express*. New York: Dell, 1986.

Donnelly, Elfie. *So Long Grandpa*. New York: Crown, 1981.

Emery, Anne. *Stepfamily*. Philadelphia, Pa.: Westminster, 1980.

Girion, Barbara. *A Tangle of Roots*. New York: Putnam, 1985.

Glass, Stuart. *A Divorce Dictionary: A Book for You and Your Children*. New York: Four Winds, 1980.

Greene, Constance C. *Beat the Turtle Drum*. New York: Dell, 1986.

Greenfield, Eloise. *Grandmama's Joy*. New York: Putnam, 1980.

Hazen, Barbara. *Tight Times*. New York: Penguin, 1983.

Helmering, Doris W. *I Have Two Families*. Nashville, Tenn.: Abingdon, 1981.

Hermes, Patricia. *Nobody's Fault*. New York: Dell, 1983.

Jones, Penelope. *Holding Together*. Scarsdale, N.Y.: Bradbury, 1981.

Krementz, Jill. *How It Feels When a Parent Dies*. New York: Knopf, 1988.

Laiken, Deidre S., and Alan J. Schneider. *Listen to Me, I'm Angry*. New York: Lothrop, 1980.

LeShan, Eda. *Learning to Say Good-By: When a Parent Dies*. New York: Macmillan, 1976.

LeShan, Eda. *What's Going to Happen to Me? When Parents Separate or Divorce*. New York: Four Winds, 1978.

Lindsay, Jeanne Warren. *Do I Have a Daddy? A Story About a Single-Parent Child*. Buena Park, Calif.: Morning Glory, 1982.

McLean, Madeena S. *My Daddy Don't Go to Work*. Minneapolis, Minn.: Carolrhoda Books, 1978.

Richards, Arlene K., and Irene Willis. *How to Get It Together When Your Parents Are Coming Apart.* New York: McKay, 1976.

Rofes, Eric, ed. *The Kids' Book of Divorce: By, For and About Kids.* New York: Random House, 1982.

Simon, Norma. *All Kinds of Families.* Chicago, Ill.: A. Whitman, 1975.

Thrasher, Crystal. *The Dark Didn't Catch Me.* New York: Macmillan, 1979.

Vigna, Judith. *She's Not My Real Mother.* Chicago, Ill.: A. Whitman, 1980.

Wright, Betty R. *My New Mom and Me.* Milwaukee, Wis.: Raintree, 1981.

For Adults

Baruth, Leroy G. *A Single Parent's Survival Guide: How to Raise the Children.* Dubuque, Iowa: Kendall-Hunt, 1979.

Beckelman, Laurie. *Homeless.* New York: Crestwood House, 1989.

Bramnick, Lea, and Anita Simon. *The Parents' Solution Book.* New York: Watts, 1983.

Capaldi, Frederick, and Barbara McRae. *Stepfamilies: A Cooperative Responsibility.* New York: Watts, 1979.

Francke, Linda B. *Growing Up Divorced.* New York: Fawcett, 1984.

Gaffney, Donna. *The Seasons of Grief.* New York: New American Library, 1988.

Gardner, Richard A. *The Parents Book about Divorce.* New York: Bantam, 1982.

Jewett, Claudia L. *Helping Children Cope with Separation and Loss.* Cambridge, Mass.: Harvard Common, 1982.

Kozol, Jonathan. *Rachel and Her Children: Homeless Families in America.* New York: Crown Publishers, 1988.

Kuczen, Barbara. *Childhood Stress: How to Raise a Healthier, Happier Child,* rev. ed. New York: Doubleday, 1987.

Laiken, Deidre. *Daughters of Divorce: The Effects of Parental Divorce on Women's Lives.* New York: Morrow, 1981.

National Collaboration for Youth. *Making the Grade: A Report Card on American Youth.* Washington, D.C. 1990.

Oakland, Thomas. *Divorced Fathers: Restructuring a Quality Life.* New York: Human Sciences, 1983.

Reed, Sally, and Craig R. Sautter. *Children of Poverty: The Status of 12 Million Young Americans.* Kappan Special Report, June 1990. Phi Delta Kappan, P.O. Box 789, Bloomington, Ind. 47402.

Ricci, Isolina. *Mom's House, Dad's House: Making Shared Custody Work*. New York: Macmillan, 1982.

Roosevelt, Ruth. *Living in Step*. New York: McGraw-Hill, 1977.

Rosenberg, Ellen. *Growing Up Feeling Good*, rev. ed. New York: Beaufort Books, 1987.

Rudolph, Marguerita. *Should the Children Know? Encounters with Death in the Lives of Children*. New York: Schocken, 1978.

Salk, Lee. *What Every Child Would Like His Parents to Know About Divorce*. New York: Harper & Row, 1978.

Schorr, Lisbeth B., and Daniel Schorr. *Within Our Reach: Breaking the Cycle of Disadvantage*. New York: Doubleday, 1989.

Segal, Julius, and Herbert Yahraes. *Child's Journey: Forces That Shape the Lives of Our Young*. New York: McGraw-Hill, 1979.

Strommen, Merton P., and Irene A. Strommen. *Five Cries of Parents*. New York: Harper & Row, 1985.

Wallerstein, Judith, and Joan Kelly. *Surviving the Breakup: How Children and Parents Cope with Divorce*. New York: Basic Books, 1982.

Ware, Ciji. *Sharing Parenthood After Divorce: An Enlightened Custody Guide*. New York: Viking, 1982.

Westoff, Leslie Aldridge. *The Second Time Around: Remarriage in America*. New York: Penguin, 1978.

Program 11/88, 12/90